ABSCISSION FERVOR

A HAIKU ANTHOLOGY

SWARNIKA

ISBN 979-888546973-9

To those who read this

Commemorate this moment

This lasts forever.

*- **Swarnika***

Contents

Contents

Contents

Contents

Preface

Originated in Japan, Haiku is a short poem with seventeen syllables distributed in three lines. The syllables are distributed in a particular pattern (5-7-5) and the poets have to adhere to it. Although non-Japanese haikus might not follow all the traditional elements closely, we've tried to keep these elements intact.

The 'kireji' (cutting word) provides structural support to the verse and allows it to stand as an independent poem. A haiku follows specific patterns while conveying complete meaning.

Working on haikus, I've comprehended that to express we don't have to always be elaborate. Sometimes concreteness speaks volumes. It is also challenging for the poets and poetesses as they have to explore the unrestrained thought within the constraint of the limited syllabic pattern and count.

This anthology consists of a total of 72+1 haikus. Each of the writers have contributed 8haikus for the book and I have written an additional haiku as its dedication.

- Swarnika

It is an ancient method of writing poems that usually consists of three lines sticking its syllables in a pattern of 5-7-5 serially in three lines. There are a few variations as well viz some poets have extended it up to four lines. However, the following Haikus have been engineered adhering to the conventional manner. As they are supposed to, the poems below attempt to capture small insinuating emotional moments of my life in a few words and a particular number of syllables.

- *Putul Mangni Mandal*

Haiku is basically a three-line Japanese poem that follows the 5-7-5 syllable pattern. I have observed that when writing a Haiku, one has to carefully choose the words not just because of limited syllable count but also the word we choose has to cover a greater meaning to it. While writing I have tried to cover different subjects, mainly concerning life, reality, social problems, and art.

- *Raman Singh*

ACKNOWLEDGEMENTS

Working on this anthology has been a wonderful experience, but it wouldn't have been the same without the dedication and contributions made by my fellow writers. This was the very first time most of them have attempted writing haikus and might I say, they exhibited initiative as well as pertinence.

I'd like to thank Gauri Shukla, Khushi Kaushik, Putul Mangni Mandal, Raman Singh, Deepanshi Ailawadi, Neeti Bhardwaj, Nishtha Trehan, and Hoilalnei Hmar for working on the haikus present in this book and sharing them with our readers.

Swarnika

Swarnika is an avid reader and an ambivert. She is a glass-half-full kind of a person, not because she is always an optimist but because she believes that a glass that is full has no more scope and ends up creating the most amount of spills.

She completed her Bachelor's and Master's degree from the University of Delhi. She has completed her three-level professional certification in Spanish from Valencia Polytechnic University, Spain. She has also completed her certificate program in French from St. Stephen's College, University of Delhi. She is currently pursuing a Post-Graduate Diploma in Business Administration from Symbiosis Centre for Distance Learning, Pune. She is working on her thesis and research papers to earn her Ph.D. degree in English Literature.

She has a keen interest in criminology and detective fiction. Writings that indulge mystery and rationale speak volumes to her. She has earned her TEFL and TESOL certificates as an English language teacher. She is also a certified dance teacher with specializations in Bharatnatyam, Kathak, and Contemporary. She is also certified in Classical Music and Fine Arts.

She exhibits abundant admiration for food and would call herself a foodie. She believes in living in the moment rather than giving the moment the opportunity to live through you without you even realizing it. She has started her company- Nrityangana Kala Kendra OPC Private Limited on her own. She has been tutoring kids along with mentoring graduate and postgraduate students in academic and creative writing.

On some days she is a dreamer while on others she is a realist. She firmly believes in humanism. Nature mesmerizes her. On a usual day, you'd find her curled up in a corner either with a book or watching a movie/episode while relishing food.

She has initiated this project and has edited the book along with compiling it.

Please hold on tightly
Because you are losing me
Tonight forever.

- *Swarnika*

II

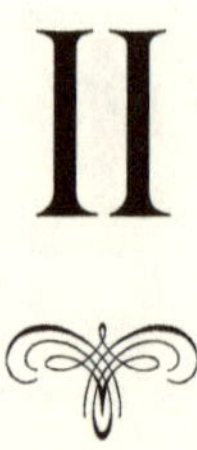

I am sorry love,
Words on lips were unspoken
Unheard we drifted.

                                   - Swarnika

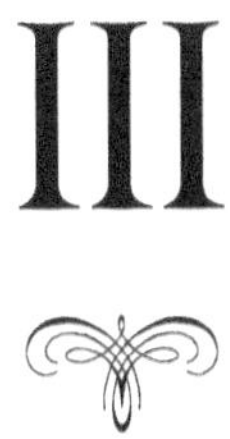

III

All these eyes on her,
She was born yesterday and
Masked her nakedness.

- *Swarnika*

IV

Coloured in day's sky
Clouded and rained love high-low
Quietly the night waits.

- Swarnika

V

Had the situation
Favoured the soul over sole
They would be alive.

- Swarnika

VI

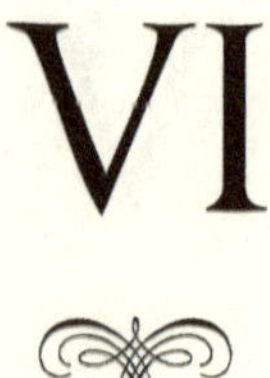

No charges filed on
The writers who murder their
Characters freely.

                    - Swarnika

VII

Your sorry cannot
Contain the angst of my heart
That breathes to its death.

- Swarnika

VIII

Heart might be in doubt
But if you still have to choose
You might lose this time.

- Swarnika

Gauri Shukla

Gauri Shukla is a third-year Literature student pursuing her passion for reading and writing from the University of Delhi. President of the Literary Society of the college, she is an avid reader who yearns to get lost in estranged, galvanic worlds of art. A national-level debater, she is someone who doesn't shy away from speaking her mind. An ardent scripturient, she has written articles for The Times of India, The Hindu, The Redstockings Chronicles, etc. She's currently working on a South-Asian anthology as an editor alongside editors from Bangladesh and Pakistan. Her main interests of study lie in Diasporic postcolonial and African- American literature. She wishes to document the experiences and sentiments of different people, belonging to different cultures, all around the world. She believes life is too short and time is fleeting thus, each moment needs to be savored and felt to its optimum level. She likes to describe herself as a wandering cloud that romances with the sky, lost yet free.

IX

The circumstances
Were not to be blamed but his
Own fragile ego.

- *Gauri Shukla*

X

The destination
Is not as adventurous
As the journey is.

- Gauri Shukla

XI

Enchanting she was,
Roaming the moonlit grim streets
Without her shadow.

- Gauri Shukla

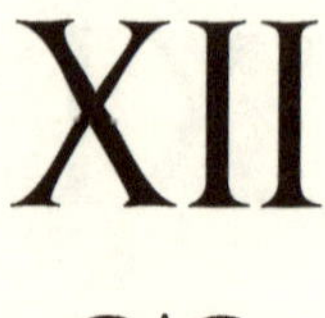

XII

The leaves turn auburn
Acting frisky with the wind,
Nature's high with Spring.

- Gauri Shukla

XIII

His ravenous hands,
Lost in gluttonous hunger
And her ignored tears.

- Gauri Shukla

XIV

Livid searing pain,
Insomnia and endless rain-
A heartbreak's sad strain.

- Gauri Shukla

XV

Coddled in blankets,
Safe from the snowy white realms
She reads all night long.

- Gauri Shukla

XVI

No destination,
Just an old road on a map
And my lover's eyes.

- Gauri Shukla

Khushi Kaushik

Khushi Kaushik, the elder child in a nuclear family, was born and brought up in Faridabad, Haryana. She studied in DAV public school, sec 14, Faridabad, and was good in studies since childhood. She had a keen interest in studying literature. The author of 'Secret of room 333' is known for her flash fiction. She started writing her first book when she was 13, which is a very young age , her interest developed in the field of content writing and she started to write poems , stories and finally decided to write a fiction . She is 20 at present and is pursuing English literature from University of Delhi. Apart from being an author she is a poetess as well and her compilation of romantic poems 'Shades of love' had a great readership. She is an eager learner and has various interests. She has a keen interest in art, she has been painting since childhood and is a very good singer as well and also has won competitions in singing . She has a dynamic personality and is someone who loves to take up new challenges and broaden her horizons.

XVII

To cry out a lake
Is strength and not a weakness
Power is to express.

- Khushi Kaushik

XVIII

People dying of dark
Still they are not paying heed
Letting smoke go on.

- *Khushi Kaushik*

XIX

They ask who am I?
I tell I am a dead fish
Living in desert.

- *Khushi Kaushik*

XX

We say its in past
And call it out in present
Destroy the future.

- Khushi Kaushik

XXI

They ask me to fly
Under the roof they provide
Hence cutting my wings.

- Khushi Kaushik

XXII

Our bad is their good
And their good can be our bad
Like yin yang we are.

- *Khushi Kaushik*

XXIII

They say they love rain
But they open umbrellas
Just love the idea.

- Khushi Kaushik

XXIV

Hanging on the strings
We all are just puppets here
Dancing by their hand.

- Khushi Kaushik

Putul Mangni Mandal

Living in New Delhi, Putul Mangni Mandal was born in December 1996. It is a pseudonym that she has adopted for the literary world. By root, her family comes from Bihar and as mentioned in the name, she belongs to the Mandal community. However, she abhors rigid statism or communism. Putul (meaning doll; it is her mother's pet name) lives with her small family of four. Financially, she is lower middle class. She studied in a government school named Sarvodaya Co. Ed. Senior Secondary in Nanak Pura. She has done her Post Graduation in English from Delhi University and aspires to become a professional writer, too, among many other possible-impossible things.

Poems have fascinated her ever since she read Kanyadān, a poem by the famous romantic Hindi writer Suryakānt Tripāthi 'Nirālā' in tenth grade. But she never knew that she could write until the day when her teacher Minākshi Mehta asked the whole class to create something. She composed her first poem Lakshya. Since then she has written many poems. Some of her English poems include On a Bus, Chores, Substitute, My Days, At Last, A Signal, and many others. She also writes in Hindi/Urdu and some of them are Intezār, Ūpar-Neechey, Bheetar, Chāl, etc. Fingers crossed, she hopes to soon come up with her poem collection. Not limiting herself to poems only, she has initiated in the field of prose writing through her first work Listen Didi which is a novella. Apart from this she also likes to write articles and essays on various literary topics.

She hopes that people will find something interesting and unique in her work. If they do so, they may use her email address given below to express their useful views.

Putulmangnimandal@gmail.com

The following poems are composed by Pooja Rai / Putul Mangni Mandal. Conceptually, they are called Haiku. It is an ancient method of writing poems that usually consists of three lines sticking its syllables in a pattern of 5-7-5 serially in three lines. There are a few variations as well viz some poets have extended it up to four lines. However, the following Haikus have been engineered adhering to the conventional manner. As they are supposed to, the poems below attempt to capture small insinuating emotional moments of my life in a few words and a particular number of syllables. But some of them like #3, #6 and #7 contains suggestive meanings as well.

XXV

Yellow crispy leaves
Spring with the frisky moments
Of dancing sparrows.

- Putul Mangni Mandal

XXVI

In the inky room
Of mine, streaks a ray and the
Room illuminates.

- Putul Mangni Mandal

XXVII

Suddenly a shriek
Of parrots penetrates through
Empty room of mine.

- Putul Mangni Mandal

XXVIII

Oh, my fridge bores me
Through the same, consistent buzz.
Don't leave me alone...

- Putul Mangni Mandal

XXIX

The growing mound of
Books are blowing my pockets.
Not money-friendly!

- *Putul Mangni Mandal*

XXX

One by one they go,
Sometimes up and sometimes low.
Thus, braids are woven.

- Putul Mangni Mandal

XXXI

There it goes again;
A trrrr-vroooom bike's cutting through a
Pigeon's colony.

- *Putul Mangni Mandal*

XXXII

Let once, abandoned
Streets listen to the children's
Giggle. They will smile.

- Putul Mangni Mandal

Raman Singh

Raman Singh was born in the year 2001 in Haryana, India. He never did things to pass time, when he held on to a thing, he gave himself completely to it. May it be playing basketball for nine years, may it be doing theatre, which also induced interest in literature. He is currently pursuing BA(Hons) in English, from Delhi University, and is an important part of the theatre society. He has also acted in six theatrical productions and has written several short plays and stories. Not to forget his love for Hindi Literature, which has added new dimensions to his imaginations and in which he finds those values and thoughts which otherwise would've been too late to discover. If there is anything else that he loves, that is a cup of coffee. His notion of feeling content and happy is to have A cup of coffee with a brownie while reading a book.

Haiku is basically a three-line Japanese poem which follow the 5-7-5 syllable pattern. I have observed that when writing a Haiku, one has to carefully choose the words not just because of limited syllable count but also that word we choose has to cover a greater meaning to it. While writing I have tried to cover different subjects, mainly concerning with life, reality, social problems, and art.

XXXIII

"This is the true world
Every other world is false"
Says, the falsest world.

- **Raman Singh**

XXXIV

Every art teaches
Madness is omnipresent
But, paintbrush matters.

- Raman Singh

XXXV

Is it fictional?
Does the false beat the truth? No
It is fictional.

- **Raman Singh**

XXXVI

A box full of sweets
In which ants enter, get trapped
It is human life.

- Raman Singh

XXXVII

Came invisibly
Took away the happiness
And left eyes with tears.

- *Raman Singh*

XXXVIII

Soared high in the sky
Trespassing all the layers
Wings shouted freedom.

- Raman Singh

XXXIX

Movements caged all life
They told me to fly now right
Can I? I replied.

- Raman Singh

XL

I felt the chill air
Pass through pores of hollow soul
But could not feel it.

- **Raman Singh**

Deepanshi Ailawadi

Deepanshi Ailawadi holds a Masters degree in English Literature. Since childhood libraries are her second home which enable her to travel across time and space. She believes each written page tells a story which should not be left unheard because at the end human beings are made up of little stories stored up in their brain's memory. Writing is one of the medium through which stories can be heard, touched and felt. Thus, she decided to write, to pay back her debt to Reading and disseminate stories which have capability to reform our ways of perception. Writing enables her to hold several personalities and perspectives in her body, sometimes she becomes a bookseller, while other times she becomes a buyer of the book and sometimes she can be both friend and enemy at once. It is this magic which tempted her to write for others and for herself too.

Following composition of poems are captured in words by Deepanshi. This kind of poetry is called Haiku, a Japanese poetic form, comprising three phrases which contains a kireji (cutting word), in a 5,7,5 pattern. It is primarily notable for its quick cinematic description of images and follows strict rhyme pattern. Following is an naive attempt to focalize life's unfocused moments.

XLI

Yesterday I saw
Myself hovering outside
My old soul's abode.

- *Deepanshi Ailawadi*

XLII

All fall down when you
Become someone else's voice
Someone else's shade.

- Deepanshi Ailawadi

XLIII

By hurting myself
I am gently trying to love
Your imprisoned flesh.

- Deepanshi Ailawadi

XLIV

Inadvertently
Past creeps into the Present
With jerky silence.

- Deepanshi Ailawadi

XLV

My plant was reborn
While quivering during storm
Every wild autumn.

- Deepanshi Ailawadi

XLVI

Offline and Online
Languorously life passes
Weak and ill signals.

- Deepanshi Ailawadi

XLVII

Memories framed on
The wall of my house breaks the
Borders of silence.

- Deepanshi Ailawadi

XLVIII

Late night every day
Algid moon heals my back and
I rose up again.

- *Deepanshi Ailawadi*

Neeti Bhardwaj

I am Neeti Bhardwaj, a student by profession who is still pursuing graduation. An overly enthusiastic person who loves to read and write whatever comes to mind. I harbor an immense passion to create artistic writings to create changes for the better in the world. I believe in a simple philosophy that takes inspiration from the minimalistic things that create a sheer impact on society without hampering the basic structure of the foundation of society.

XLIX

Fall of the Last Tree,
Shook the world underneath it;
Left the world astound.

- *Neeti Bhardwaj*

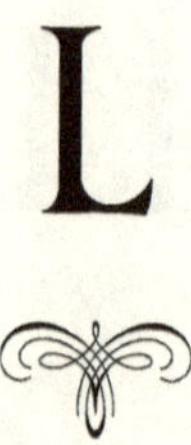

My soul torn and reaped
Hollow it is underneath
Leave it alone please.

- Neeti Bhardwaj

LI

The wind shook the tree
As if dancing along it
The leaves fell with grace.

- *Neeti Bhardwaj*

LII

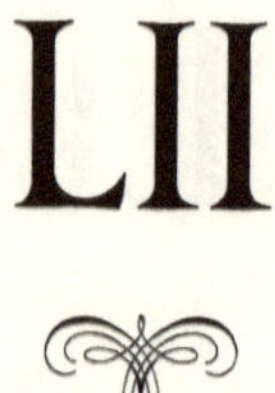

Rain poured heavily
Drops falling on the windshield
Left me in deep thought.

- Neeti Bhardwaj

LIII

Sand spread across beach
Walking with a heavy heart
Left footprints of past.

- Neeti Bhardwaj

LIV

A child without love
Is like flower without soil
It withers and dies.

- Neeti Bhardwaj

LV

Flamingos go far
To find their own home and love
To spend their life with.

- Neeti Bhardwaj

LVI

The butterfly waits
In its cocoon, wanting to
See the world up close.

- Neeti Bhardwaj

Nishtha Trehan

Nishtha Trehan is a student at Atma Ram Sanatan Dharma College, University of Delhi, studying English Honours. In her breaks, she likes to read, write, and journal. It is under the guidance of her supervisor, Swarnika, that she has been able to finish these haikus.

LVII

The blood will thicken
Water will heal and listen
Ice will not forgive.

- Nishtha Trehan

LVIII

Once the chapter ends
Your story is not over
Just pick another.

- *Nishtha Trehan*

LIX

Gazing at the stars
Standing on the precipice
You begin to hope.

- Nishtha Trehan

LX

Just like a phoenix
The wounded soldier rises
His fire never quenched.

- *Nishtha Trehan*

LXI

Words reside in you
There's a yearning that exists
For all that's unknown.

- *Nishtha Trehan*

LXII

My insides combine
Resurrected once again
And you are the cause.

- *Nishtha Trehan*

LXIII

As the sun departs
Terrible truths are confessed
Moonlight is tender.

- Nishtha Trehan

LXIV

Only ghosts I know
Are the relics of my past
And I am the ash.

- *Nishtha Trehan*

Hoilalnei Hmar

Hoilalnei Hmar is a college student from Rajdhani College, Delhi University. Currently residing in Manipur, she is a feminist. Not to mention, she had a very interesting life in high school where she graduated from Christ Jyoti School, Mantripukhri (Imphal). She worked on herself and evolved herself as a better person when she attended Don Bosco Higher Secondary School, Maram(Manipur).

LXV

The wind hibernate
The sun that goes down again
Brings a new day too.

- Hoilalnei Hmar

LXVI

A day beautiful
Am so sure when to enjoy
The hay of sunshine.

- *Hoilalnei Hmar*

In a small vast world
I am excited about
The tomorrow plan.

- Hoilalnei Hmar

LXVIII

My belly is full
But I love eating so much
That I would not care.

- *Hoilalnei Hmar*

LXIX

Loving myself where
I cannot stop smiling at
Myself when I look.

- *Hoilalnei Hmar*

LXX

Wise is where heart goes
Beats for everyone else and
Not mind opinion.

- Hoilalnei Hmar

LXXI

Sun shining brightly
And moon shines brighter at night
That is how days pass.

- *Hoilalnei Hmar*

LXXII

Death becomes us but
We go different ways so
Be kind and do good.

- Hoilalnei Hmar

THANK YOU!

Dear Reader,

I'd like to thank you for reading Abscission Fervor. I really hope you could appreciate the work done by all the co-authors of this anthology. I'd love to hear your feedback. If you'd like to reach out you can drop in an email at swara@nrityanganakalakendra.com.

Regards,
Swarnika